MORE THAN FAMILY:

NON-FAMILY EXECUTIVES IN THE FAMILY BUSINESS

Craig E. Aronoff, Ph.D.
John L. Ward, Ph.D.

Family Business Leadership Series, No. 13

Business Owner Resources
1220-B Kennestone Circle
P.O. Box 4356
Marietta, Georgia 30061-4356

ISSN: 1071-5010
ISBN: 1-891652-03-6
© 2000

Family Business Leadership Series

We believe that family businesses are special, not only to the families that own and manage them but to our society and to the private enterprise system. Having worked and interacted with hundreds of family enterprises in the past twenty years, we offer the insights of that experience and the collected wisdom of the world's best and most successful family firms.

This volume is a part of a series offering practical guidance for family businesses seeking to manage the special challenges and opportunities confronting them.

To order additional copies, contact:
Business Owner Resources
1220-B Kennestone Circle
Post Office Box 4356
Marietta, Georgia 30061-4356
Tel: 1-800-551-0633
Web Sites: www.fbop.com/www.family-business.net

Quantity discounts are available.

Other volumes in the series include:

Family Business Succession: The Final Test of Greatness

Family Meetings: How to Build a Stronger Family and a Stronger Business

Another Kind of Hero: Preparing Successors For Leadership

How Families Work Together

Family Business Compensation

How to Choose & Use Advisors: Getting the Best Professional Family Business Advice

Financing Transitions: Managing Capital and Liquidity in the Family Business

Family Business Governance: Maximizing Family and Business Potential

Preparing Your Family Business For Strategic Change

Making Sibling Teams Work: The Next Generation

Developing Family Business Policies: Your Guide to the Future

Family Business Values: How to Assure a Legacy of Continuity and Success

Contents

Exhibits

I. *Introduction: A Fruitful Collaboration*

One of the greatest challenges to family business growth is the willingness and ability to depend on executives who are not family members. Whether non-family executives are hired from outside the company or promoted from within, the issues are much the same: Choosing the right person for the job and managing him or her in such a way as to mutually benefit the company and the non-family executive.

All growing family businesses eventually face the need to attract top-level talent from outside of the family. The business will need the energy and ideas that only outsiders can provide. Indeed, according to our research, about 12 percent of family-owned businesses have had persons outside the family serve as CEO.

This booklet is designed to help business owners become more knowledgeable about attracting and retaining valuable non-family managers. It will help you to understand how non-family executives can help you grow your business and assure its survival to the next generation. It offers guidance on hiring or promoting the right people for executive positions and managing them effectively so that they will want to stay with your company and give it their all. Chapter IV, "Making Non-Family Executives A Part Of Your Team," for example, tells you what non-family executives want and offers suggestions for meeting their needs so that they can meet yours. You will also find advice here on developing good relationships between your children and your non-family executives.

Family business owners need to understand what it's like to be a key player in a family company but not a member of the family. As often as possible, this booklet presents the perspectives of non-family executives so that family business owners can interact more successfully on matters like compensation, making the transition to the next generation, and professionalizing the company. Chapter VIII, for example, is addressed directly to non-family executives, but it is also intended for family business owners and managers, board members, next generation leaders and others who are invested in their family business's future. It will help non-family executives more clearly understand their roles in a family business and how to manage those roles and work with the family successfully. Conversely, it will help the family, the board, and others understand what it's like to be in the position of a non-family executive.

We believe that all existing or prospective non-family executives in family businesses should read this booklet. Just as you as a family business owner gain an understanding of them from these pages, so will they gain an understanding of you and your needs, your fears and desires. We hope that as a result, you and your non-family executives learn to communicate with each other more effectively, better understand the expectations you have of each other, and achieve — and enjoy — long-lasting, productive working relationships that take your company forward.

To grow and achieve long-term success, a family business depends on a fruitful collaboration between the business-owning family and its non-family executives. As Charles E. "Gus" Whalen, Jr., president of the Warren Featherbone Company, a family business in Gainesville, GA, once warned in a *Harvard Business Review* article, once a family firm runs out of competent family members, "you're out of business" — unless, of course, you turn to non-family talent.

"In short," he said, **"you need to find and help develop new heroes for your business."**

That's what this booklet is about: encouraging you and helping you to create new heroes for your business — heroes from outside the family to complement the heroes within.

II. *A Delicate Relationship: Family Business Owners And Non-Family Executives*

Family business leaders are frequently resistant to and uneasy about putting non-family members into key executive positions. Talented executives are often equally cautious about joining family firms, even though they see many benefits of doing so.

The family business leaders have their reasons: They often see a non-family executive as a cost, rather than an investment in the business. Entrepreneurs often have a hard time accepting that good talent earns great returns. Sometimes, they worry that the non-family managers will not be as loyal and trustworthy and hardworking as family members are, or that having people outside the family in key positions will dilute the family's power or role in decision-making or erode the values so important to the company culture and to the family. They wonder about the effect of non-family executives on the career paths of younger family members.

They fret over the notion that a non-family executive will want equity in the company. They experience anxiety over how well non-family executives will get along with the next generation of family members in the business, or non-active family owners. And what kind of relationship will top family executives themselves have with these outsiders? How can you be sure non-family managers will do what you want them to do? What if they want

You deserve the best. Not only that, the best of the best want to work for family firms.

you to change the way you conduct business? And what about the horror stories the business owners have heard about non-family executives who try to wrest control from the family or who go off and start competing businesses, or worse?

Non-family employees who have just become executives in a family business or are thinking about joining a family firm have concerns of their own. Will they be treated on a par with family executives? Will their ideas be heard and will they be given a chance to make a difference — or will the family call all the shots on how the business is to be run? Will they be given an opportunity to advance in the company, or is there a "glass ceiling" for non-family employees?

They've heard their own horror stories — about what it's like to work in a family firm where family members are at one another's throats and want non-family executives to take sides, or where non-family executives are expected to help resolve family conflicts. They've also heard about autocratic founders who want you to jump when they say jump, and about family firms that don't follow best business practices. What if, for example, a talented non-family executive is expected to work amiably with an incompetent family manager, someone who is in an executive position only because he or she is "family"?

Family business owners and non-family executives both have a lot of legitimate concerns about working with each other. However, we believe wholeheartedly that these relationships can work for the good of all concerned, including the business itself. We have seen it happen over and over again.

Our decades of experience in working with family businesses has led us to some simple but important conclusions: **You deserve the best. Not only that, the best of the best want to work for family firms. Finally, you should expect nothing less than the very best performance from your non-family executives**.

In survey after survey, managing non-family executives ranks in the top three areas of concern for family business owners. This is a complex issue. It's an area that requires a big investment of your time and salary dollars, and — if it works out — it can yield an excellent return on your investment. You are not alone in your search for answers to questions about managing key non-family executives. That's why we wrote this booklet.

Recognize the Benefits

As a family business leader, and especially if you're the CEO, the place to start is to recognize the many ways that non-family executives benefit a family business. As we pointed out in the introduction, non-family executives enable your business to grow. If executive positions were limited to family members, the business would be narrowly confined and, by necessity, would have to stay small. **Business growth requires a larger, deeper pool of qualified management talent than any one family can realistically produce.**

Business growth requires a larger, deeper pool of qualified management talent than any one family can realistically produce.

In addition, good, well-chosen, and wisely-managed non-family executives help your company keep its competitive edge. Hardworking professional non-family managers set an example for other employees to follow, including up and coming family members. If they come from other companies, they bring to your business

4

the knowledge, experience and discipline that they gained elsewhere.

Furthermore, your company gains the advantage of their ideas, ideas that you might not come by if you limit your executive team to an inner circle of family members. Any company can benefit from diversity of thinking, and when fresh ideas come from outside the family and decision making is shared with talented non-family people, your company stands a better chance of keeping an innovative edge and meeting its strategic challenges.

EXHIBIT 1 ▰▰▰▰▰▰▰▰▰▰▰▰▰▰▰▰▰

Why Non-Family Executives Want To Work For a Family Firm

— Being close to the seat of power can be more fun than being *in* the seat of power.

— A family business may offer more responsibility and more opportunity to make a difference.

— Admiration and respect for the family's values and culture.

— Commitment to the family business's exciting mission.

— Opportunity to work in a non-bureaucratic environment.

— Opportunity to build wealth for oneself.

— Family-friendly attitude toward employees.

Beyond these broad and vital benefits, our experience tells us and research shows that non-family executives can play a number of valuable roles in a family firm. These include, but are not limited to, the following:

— Serving as an alter ego or "consigliere" to the founder/CEO. In this role, the non-family manager embraces the family and its culture and values as if they were his or her own. While complementing the CEO's skills, he/she also promotes the family culture to non-family employees and assures them that the family is trustworthy, solid, and strong. This can be a very powerful role to play, one we like to describe as "part warrior, part pastor."

— Serving as strategic planners and implementers. Founders tend to work in spurts of creative genius and need stable implementers who can pick up the pieces, transfer the strategy to other people, and build support for ideas. Non-family executives in this role can also surface disturbing data of value to the organization ("That person you hired that you were so keen about isn't really working out.")

— Supporting the succession process in a variety of ways. These might include mentoring the next generation and helping to prepare it for leadership, or serving as a bridge between generations when an heir is not available to take over. Sometimes the non-family executive even catalyzes the process. (We go into this in more detail in Chapter V.)

— Being an insurance policy. If something happens to the chief executive — a serious illness or an accident, for example — a trusted non-family executive can step in and run the company until the CEO's return.

— Serving as an "adoptive" son or daughter. When business owners have no successors, they may want the emotional satisfaction of having somebody that they like and believe in growing into the leadership position. So sometimes, there's a very constructive and special relationship that builds up between an entrepreneur and a non-family manager.

All of these roles offer a measure of comfort to business owners. They get the reassurance that they and their families don't have to go it alone and that there are smart people by their side to help them meet the difficult challenges of running a family firm.

What Attracts Outsiders

You've heard the old joke: "I wouldn't want to be the member of any club that would accept me." Sometimes family business owners are like that — they get suspicious of non-family executives who would want to join a family firm. A business owner simply may not understand the motives of someone who can't ever expect to be CEO of the company.

Yet, many "outsiders" find family businesses attractive places to work. Not every talented manager wants to be a CEO. For some, particularly those with low ego needs, it's more fun to be close to the seat of power rather than in it. Many non-family executives see, in family businesses, an opportunity to build personal wealth. Some are attracted by the opportunity to have broader responsibilities than they might get somewhere else. Others are attracted to a family firm's exciting mission, its non-bureaucratic nature, or its family-friendly attitude toward employees. Others are drawn by respect and admiration or the owning family's values and culture.

EXHIBIT 2 ██

What Good Non-Family Managers Can Do For Your Company

— Enable the family business to grow.

— Enhance standards of professionalism.

— Bring in ideas that help the company stay innovative and competitive.

— Serve as the CEO's alter ego, complementing the chief's skills.

— Transfer the family's values and ideas to other employees.

— Strengthen the company by assisting with decision making and strategic planning.

— Mentor the next generation.

— Support the succession-planning process.

— Serve as an "insurance policy," running the company if something befalls the CEO.

And to some, **family companies committed to long-term private ownership look increasingly secure in this fast-paced world.**

However, as some of the fears of non-family executives discussed above suggest, they leave family businesses for a variety of reasons: when the family engages in destructive nepotism, placing family members in jobs just because they are family members, not because they are qualified; or the family abuses the business, using employees to take care of personal chores at an owner's home for example. Non-family executives also leave if they perceive an inequity of rewards that grossly favor family members over outsiders. Sometimes they leave because they don't fit in with the culture of the family business, or because the family closes itself to innovation and change and fails to stay competitive.

The many reasons that non-family executives leave a business suggest that **companies that want and need to go outside the family to**

EXHIBIT 3 ████████████████████████████████████

Why Non-Family Executives Leave

— Insufficient opportunity for advancement and growth.

— Poor fit with the family business culture.

— Abuse of the business by the family.

— Lack of opportunity to create personal wealth.

— Can't make a difference because new ideas and change are resisted.

— Destructive nepotism.

---

fill executive posts must prepare themselves for the experience. That means opening themselves up to change, dedicating themselves to being as professional in their practices as they can be, and being prepared to give up some control and power in return for greater business success. It also means regarding non-family executives as investments, not costs. You can rarely have too many good, well-managed people, whether they're family members or not. And they will nearly always provide a handsome return on your investment.

III. *Striking The Right Match*

It's a commonly held myth that business founders are confident, dynamic go-getters who are charging up the hill every minute of the day. Our perception, however, is that entrepreneurs are often humble people whose sense of self-worth can be lower than it should be. They are modest, and modest people tend to under-hire.

One of our missions is to convince you, the family business leader, that you deserve the best managers, and you can get them.

A business leader's attitude has a great impact on a company's ability to attract and retain excellent managers. In the first generation particularly, when the founder is in charge, there may be some psychological hurdles to overcome—among them being the modesty we've described above.

We find that business owners often are suspicious of talented people. They worry that excellent, intelligent managers will judge them harshly, and that such executives will pressure them to conform to standard management practices. Owners also worry that they need to please talented people to keep them.

In addition, research supports the notion that entrepreneurial personalities display a tremendous need for control and a desire to be at the center of things. As a result, they hire people who won't challenge their control.

Family business owners also tend to avoid the use of search firms and industrial psychologists when they're hiring executive talent. Search firms are seen as not only expensive, but they also won't let you be ambiguous. And if you can't be ambiguous, you have to say what you really want! That's hard for a lot of business owners.

> *A business leader's attitude has a great impact on a company's ability to attract and retain excellent managers.*

We also find that family businesses exhibit an enormous tendency to hire people who are looking for jobs, rather than seeking people who are already happily employed and doing great at their current jobs. Needless to say, the latter make far better candidates.

Many business owners simply don't like the whole business of hiring. They dread the process of recruiting people and negotiating compensation. They don't feel confident about assessing people. They've

been burned by past hiring mistakes. They understand that a mistake leads to another dreaded situation: Letting someone go.

Once hires are made, family businesses often do not adequately train and develop employees for future roles, thus limiting the company's ability to promote from within to executive levels. Let's suppose you need to fill an executive slot with a non-family employee. Of course, we encourage promoting from within, if possible. Promoting from within means that you have had an opportunity to observe the candidate over time. You already know that he or she is capable and loyal and trustworthy and fits into the corporate culture. What's more, if you've done your job, you've already developed the candidate for this new role. The inside candidate also already understands the dynamics of your family business.

While sometimes you have no other choice, hiring an outside executive is riskier because such issues as loyalty, trustworthiness, and shared values have yet to be tested. Furthermore, bringing somebody in from the outside can be disruptive and time consuming, as the new executive learns the ropes, scrambles to earn the trust of a whole new set of personalities, and perhaps struggles to cope with the realities of working in a family firm.

An important part of finding a good fit is being sure that a non-family candidate holds values that are similar to those of the business-owning family.

Values Are Key

What should a family business be looking for in its non-family executives? Like any company, a family firm needs executives with talent and skill to meet the demands of the position. This may mean superb ability to lead others and a solid knowledge of the company's products or services.

In a family company, however, **an important part of finding a good fit is being sure that a non-family candidate holds values that are similar to those of the business-owning family** and the business culture. Even though one candidate for a top job appeared to share values that the business-owning family held dear, the company put him through a battery of psychological tests. "They reinforced our impressions that he was a good person, an honest person, and a very high-energy, intelligent person," said one of the family owners.

Many business owners ask their spouses to meet the candidate to

EXHIBIT 4

Non-Family Managers: An Expense Or An Investment?

Business owners who see non-family managers as an expense tend to:

■ Hire people desperately needed "this minute" to fill an open spot.

■ Under-hire.

■ Under-invest in training.

■ Shun outside help in hiring.

■ Hire people who are looking for jobs.

■ May not be making money on every employee they hire.

Business owners who see non-family managers as an investment tend to:

■ Hire people to build for future roles.

■ Groom and develop people for more challenging responsibilities.

■ Set aside an adequate percentage of their budget for training and development.

■ Utilize search firms and industrial psychologists to help them make the best choices.

■ Seek out people who are already employed and doing great in their jobs.

■ Expect to make money on every employee.

get a valuable, often instinctively insightful, opinion.
Additionally, when you are conducting your search, you will want to:

☛ **Seek people who complement the abilities of family executives.**
You want to multiply the talents of the company, not duplicate them.
You will need people who have abilities that are not available within
the family.

☛ **Look for a prospective employee who will have credibility not
just in the business but in the family.** Family members who are not
directly involved in the business need to feel that the non-family executives are people they can trust — particularly if they are in top positions.

☛ **Consider the candidate's ability to teach or to play a role in the
succession process.** More often than not, you'll want your non-family
executives to mentor and coach the younger members of the family.
You'll want people who can serve as role models and who will help map
out a development plan that will prepare your sons and daughters for
leadership positions — including the top leadership position.

☛ **Don't go it alone.** Use other top executives, industrial psychologists,
and independent board members to aid with the hiring decision. While
they don't make the final decision, they can be helpful in confirming
your judgment or raising "red flags."

☛ **Make use of family-business advisors**. "Family-business professionals can assist you in making sure that you put together the appropriate
compensation package and employment agreement to motivate a new
person and to accomplish the goals that you want accomplished," said
one family business co-owner. She and her husband hired a CEO for their
company and, in the process, drew on the services of a family-business
consultant and their attorney who specializes in family businesses.

☛ **Expect some loss of privacy.** When you bring non-family people
into senior-level positions, they need access to all the company's rel-
evant financial data to make good decisions. They'll also see a lot of
what goes on in the family. In addition to all the other considerations
you must make when hiring, you'll want to look for people with whom
you feel personally comfortable.

One family business we know invites the candidate and spouse to dinner at their home as a part of the selection process. They pay special
attention to how "family friendly" and caring the candidate is.

Understand Expectations

It's important to the future success of the relationship between family members and non-family executives that expectations on both sides are out on the table before a hire or promotion is completed. Clarifying expectations reduces misunderstandings and helps ward off disappointment. It's fair of managerial candidates to want a written job description. They need to know what informal roles are expected of them as well as what their formal duties and responsibilities are. They need to know the limits of their power, what criteria will be used to judge their performance, and what compensation they can expect. They need to understand what career path is available to them and how high they can go in the company. It is also helpful to the process to provide candidates with copies of family and business mission and values statements, family employment policies, and other documents that give candidates an in-depth picture of the environment in which they will be working.

It's important to the future success of the relationship between family members and non-family executives that expectations on both sides are out on the table before a hire or promotion is completed. Clarifying expectations reduces misunderstandings and helps ward off disappointment.

The candidates themselves should be equally forthcoming about their own desires and expectations. What are their career goals? If they want to run a company someday, for example, your family firm might not be the place for them — unless you and the candidate agree that he or she can make a valuable contribution during the next five years and then move on. What are the candidate's compensation expectations, and can you meet them? What do the candidates expect to contribute to your company, and what kind of experience do they hope to gain? What are the candidates' values and are they complementary with those of the family and the company?

Turnover Has Its Good Side

Jim O., a 56-year-old business owner, learned that his 45-year-old administrative vice president would be leaving. He would become executive vice president of a similar firm owned by one of Jim's friends in another state. Jim congratulated his employee and called his friend to tell him that he had hired a good person.

Charlie L. faced a similar situation, but when he found out, he lectured his departing operations manager about loyalty. He offered a 10-percent raise and promised the employee that if he would stay, a higher position would open up.

What Jim realizes — and Charlie does not — is that turnover can be good for a family business.

Most family business owners tend to be like Charlie. Since starting their businesses, they have struggled and suffered with a shortage of good people. When key employees leave, family members have to pick up the slack themselves, returning to duties they thought they had put behind them.

As a business strengthens, it can better endure turnover. But most business owners prefer to avoid turnover altogether. "What could be more valuable to our business than our employees' commitment?" they reason. Overpaying long-term people to reward their loyalty is a common practice in family businesses because it saves the agony and cost of replacing them. But there is a hidden danger.

As a business matures, its growth rate slows. Time, employee loyalty, and retention inevitably conspire to reduce opportunities to add new people.

When Charlie's business was young and growing, he built a team of like-minded people seeking opportunities. As the business matured, the managers aged together. With the company's executives all about the same age, how much room is there for younger people, including Charlie's children, to be promoted? With mature executives reinforcing each other's views, how receptive might they be to new ideas or changes?

As a business strengthens, it can better endure turnover. But most business owners prefer to avoid turnover altogether.

Our experience is that this situation results in organizational stagnation. To see whether your business might suffer similar problems, make a drawing of your organization chart as a pyramid of ages. Charlie's business might look like this:

CHARLIE'S PYRAMID ▽

Because Charlie's business is overloaded with mature executives who are some years from retirement, there can be no movement. In time, several concurrent retirements will leave the company with too few people eligible for promotion into key positions.

Charlie will wonder what happened to initiative, ideas, and energy. He'll be even more upset if his son is the next employee who gets frustrated and leaves. That is the price of too little turnover.

Consider Jim's organizational profile, however. It looks like this:

JIM'S PYRAMID

While Jim's company is run by mature top management, several younger people are being tested for potential. As senior executives retire, several candidates are available for promotion from within. New ideas are in good supply, and the vast majority of the managers don't have a vested interest in the status quo.

There's another advantage. Jim has two children among six in middle management in the lowest age bracket. They have a peer group to work with and to be compared with. They have older, intervening managers who can help them sharpen their skills. They can experience orderly development and follow a career path to the top of the organization.

How can your company be more like Jim's? The answer is turnover — planned, accepted turnover.

Start with the middle managers. Assess them not on their past contributions but on their clear potential for top management. If that potential is lacking, now is the time for them to find other jobs. As the years pass, finding a new position becomes more difficult. They are likely to stagnate — and your business will too.

A company can't expect to keep all of its younger managers. Consequently, more are needed than there are positions above them to fill.

Obviously, you will seek only very good people. Some will leave for better opportunities. Therefore, there should be turnover of good people. Having good young people recruited away to other companies isn't an insult. It's a compliment. Imagine if no one wanted any of your people. The key is to keep the very best.

Our ideal is a nice, evolutionary progression. Several good younger people, including your children, are hired, and the best ones move up as middle managers are promoted to executive positions that become vacant through retirement. A good organization is prepared for the future, and the family successor has a good team in place when he or she takes over.

Developing executive talent requires vision, energy, and courage. The organizational pyramid has to be imagined many years ahead. Recruiting, performance reviews, and coaching have to be taken seriously. Since loyalty and stability are highly valued in family businesses, it takes courage to implement programs that shake up people (as turnover inevitably does), even if it is in the best future interests of the company and its employees.

Turnover of good people can be a good thing. Obviously, you want to keep the very best for yourself. But you can't recognize the best unless you have several candidates to compare — candidates who have had ample opportunity to grow in your organization.

Redefining Loyalty

Family business owners tend to highly value and reward loyalty on the part of their employees and try to give it in return. But to maintain management vitality, the business needs to reward performance, contribution, and innovation more than length of service.

Some turnover of middle-aged and older executives is desirable, maybe essential. A better definition of employer loyalty may become: to assure each employee the opportunity to grow to his or her fullest potential and to assure that inevitable outplacements are managed with dignity and respect.

EXHIBIT 5 ▮▮▮▮▮▮▮▮▮▮▮▮▮▮▮▮▮▮▮▮▮▮▮▮▮

How To Get The Best Non-Family Managers (And Keep Them)

1. Remember: You deserve the best.

2. Take advantage of outside help, such as search firms and industrial psychologists.

3. Be sure your expectations of each other are explicit and compatible.

4. Seek people who are better at what they do than you.

5. As a company, have clear, open goals that have been agreed on by owners and management.

6. Look for candidates with values similar to those held by the family and the company.

7. Design a compensation package that rewards performance and provides an opportunity to create personal wealth.

8. Make clear that next-generation family members will have to earn their place.

9. Demonstrate that non-family executives are business peers of the family, not the "hired help."

10. Give non-family executives responsibility worthy of their talents.

11. Create a career path for non-family employees.

12. Make sure a certain percentage of executives and new hires are from outside the family.

The Right Mix

Building a senior management team that includes talented people from both within and outside the family clearly means more than finding individuals with the right skill sets for the jobs available.

That's important, obviously, but it's just as important that family business owners look for people with values that match those of the family and who will fit in comfortably with the corporate culture. It's also important that the mix represent a diversity of backgrounds, perspectives, and ages so that the management group combines the wisdom of experience with the freshest of ideas. Such a combination can keep your company on the cutting edge for a long time to come.

IV: *Making Non-Family Executives A Part of Your Team*

One of the surest ways to retain talented non-family managers and to increase their value to your company as time goes on is to make them a full-fledged part of your team — whether they are mature senior executives or younger, lower-level managers with the potential to handle greater responsibility.

Non-family executives must consider their *own* families' best interests. It is up to you to convince them that their families' best interests and the greatest rewards lie in serving *your* family business. It is unrealistic to expect non-family key people to exhibit blind loyalty.

What makes non-family executives feel like they're part of the team? The short answer is: Being treated on a par with family managers, and being honored with responsibility, respect, recognition, and good relationships with family members. Here, in more detail, are what non-family managers need in order to feel a member of your team, with our suggestions for how you can meet those needs:

— Non-family executives want responsibility commensurate with their talent and they want a chance to make a difference. To accommodate those desires, it's necessary to create a career path for non-family executives just as you would for family members. This means analyzing your business and asking yourself if there's room for your non-family executives to assume more responsibility over time. Is your business designed to accommodate both the family members who are coming along as well as the non-family executives? Is it clear to non-family people that they can aspire to the very highest levels of your organization? Can they see enough movement, enough promotion at a fast-enough rate, and enough variety of opportunity to make your company interesting and worthwhile to them? Or is it evident to them that non-family people are choked out

> *What makes non-family executives feel like they're part of the team? The short answer is: Being treated on a par with family managers, and being honored with responsibility, respect, recognition, and good relationships with family members.*

because of an over-abundance of family members?

Families address this challenge in a number of ways. Some stipulate that only a given percentage of top jobs — a third, for example — will be held by family members. Others take the position that "we have to have more divisions or departments than we have family members to head them, so that we have opportunities for non-family executives to run profit centers for our company. We want our non-family employees to believe that there's an opportunity here for them to get into a level of very important responsibility where they can show their own value, create their own profit, and achieve excellence." Families with these attitudes know that they have to really grow their businesses to have room for the non-family executives.

Large businesses owned by modest-sized families will probably have little trouble providing opportunities for talented outsiders. But in smaller businesses, making room for non-family executives can be difficult, especially when there are several family members eager to move up. That's when a family employment policy outlining the rules of family members' participation in the business can be an especially useful tool. It can be designed to raise the bar even higher for family members to join and rise in the business, making sure that only the most qualified are absorbed into the enterprise. (See *Developing Family Business Policies: Your Guide to the Future*, No. 11 in the Family Business Leadership Series.)

— Non-family executives want a good relationship with your children. Laying a foundation for good relationships begins when the children are very young and you teach them to respect the non-family employees in your business. As your children are growing, you need to communicate to them and reinforce the truths that the family is indebted to its non-family workforce and that they are of great importance and value to the business.

Prepare your children for working with non-family employees. Remind them that, like family members, non-family employees have a stake in the company's success. Help them to understand how much they can learn from key non-family executives and encourage them to take advantage of the opportunity.

Don't interfere when there is a conflict between one of

Don't interfere when there is a conflict between one of your children and a non-family executive. Encourage your children to try to work things out on their own.

20

your children and a non-family executive. Encourage your children to try to work things out on their own.

Make clear to your children what expectations you have of the non-family executives who are supervising them. If you have told your sales vice president that he's to go harder on your son, Kurt, than on the non-family members of the sales staff, then Kurt needs to hear that from you. He needs to understand that you are instructing managers to hold young family members to a higher standard so that they, the next generation, can earn respect throughout the company. Otherwise, Kurt will begin to resent his non-family boss and conflict may erupt unnecessarily.

Set an example for your children. When they see you treating non-family executives with respect and fairness, they'll follow your lead.

There's a natural tendency toward competitiveness between ambitious family members and non-family employees. A CEO may tell his daughter, Jennifer, that she's not going to get the top position unless she earns it. Jennifer realizes that if she's not chosen, the most likely successor to lead the company is one of the non-family key executives. The best way to minimize contentiousness is through thoughtful team-building at the executive level, making sure that both family and non-family members have significant roles to play and understand that they are valued.

Above all, set an example for your children. When they see you treating non-family executives with respect and fairness, they'll follow your lead.

— Non-family executives want to know where they stand, and they want to be treated fairly. To meet both of those important needs, we suggest three steps: (1) Share your succession plans; (2) Have a family employment policy and share it with your key non-family managers; and (3) Develop a compensation policy that applies to all employees.

We get more deeply into the topic of succession in Chapter V. Suffice it to say here that if the family's intention is that only a family member can become CEO, your non-family executives need to know that as soon as you know it, and potential hires need to be told up-front. Shutting off access to the top position may discourage some candidates from coming to work for you. Some of your more ambitious non-family executives may leave. However, some form of "golden handcuffs" may help you retain a valued executive, and other incentives, discussed in Chapter VII, may prove attractive to potential hires.

We advise having a family employment policy because it tells the non-family executives what rules govern the entry of family members into the business, including the requirements they must meet and preparations they must make. **A family employment policy proves to the non-family executive that the family takes very seriously the issue of family members joining the business, and that family members must meet high standards to earn the privilege of joining and being promoted.** Non-family executives can take some measure of comfort from the fact that the awarding of positions in the company is based on merit for family members as well as for non-family employees.

Like the family employment policy, a compensation policy that applies to all employees will reassure your non-family executives that your family is thoughtful and fair and is trying to run the company in an objective, businesslike manner. Simply put, a compensation policy is your philosophy of compensation. It answers the question, "How do we pay our people?" Some families choose to pay the market rate for each job. They may use a compensation consultant or industry surveys to establish what the market rates are. Other families may use a board of directors compensation committee to establish and guide compensation policy.

What's important is that a general philosophy and procedures, or system, be set forth to govern compensation issues, including bonuses and other incentives, within a company. There should be no perception of inequity between non-family and family executives related to the rewards of employment.

A family employment policy proves to the non-family executive that the family takes very seriously the issue of family members joining the business, and that family members must meet high standards to earn the privilege of joining and being promoted.

— **Non-family key executives want to be involved in strategic planning and decision making.** In a very real sense, you need to share power with your key non-family executives. Participation in strategic planning should not be the preserve of family members only or just the CEO. When you bring non-family executives into the process, you not only get "buy-in," or support, from them for the decisions that are made, you also get the benefit of the fresh, broader ideas that they can bring to the table.

If you do not include non-family key executives in the process, you may be sending the message that they are not in your business to think, they are in it to do what you tell them to do. When that happens, you lose the special benefits that accrue from having good, non-family managers.

— Non-family executives need you to share information and communicate openly with them.
To build trust with non-family executives and demonstrate that you regard them as professionals, you need to share information with them. That includes information that you no doubt regard as sensitive — profit-and-loss statements, knowledge of what family members who work for them and other subordinates are earning, and the like. On a more personal level, this

The best family businesses we know are those where the family takes the attitude that "we owe our employees and we owe our key executives more than they owe us." And their actions match their attitude.

means your senior non-family managers will also have some knowledge of the family and its problems. Honest, human vulnerability builds a special relationship of trust.

Keeping non-family managers informed and communicating openly with them may stretch your comfort level. But in the long run, it will be worth the stretch.

— Non-family executives want to be listened to and heard. Again, they want to make a contribution to your organization and they want to make a difference. When you respect them by listening to them and adopting their good ideas or following their advice, you are letting them know they are of value to your family and your company. In return, their excitement about the company and their pride in it are enhanced and so is their motivation.

— Non-family executives need praise and recognition. There are many ways of sharing family business success with non-family executives and one of the simplest and most important is openly and generously to share credit for the accomplishments of the business. As Robert Woodruff, legendary leader of the Coca-Cola Company, liked to say, "You can accomplish anything as long as you don't care who gets the credit for it." **The best family businesses we know are those where the family takes the attitude that "we owe our employees and we owe our key executives more than they owe us." And their actions match their attitude.**

— **Key non-family executives need to have a relationship with the world outside your door.** Unless the non-family executive is the company CEO, he or she typically would not sit on the board and probably would not have a formal relationship with board members. Nevertheless, independent directors can serve as valuable mentors. Non-family executives can take real pleasure from being around and learning from outside directors. The mere fact that there is an independent board can play a role in attracting and retaining non-family executives — they will see the existence of such a board as further evidence that the family holds itself accountable, is open to input, will share information, and will think about things objectively.

The relationship of non-family executives to vendors, banks, and customers should not be any different in a family business than it is in any other business. However, we find that family business owners often shelter non-family employees from the outside world. They may discourage non-family managers from being exposed to professional education events, getting involved in community leadership roles, or having relationships with customers and suppliers, based on the notion that these are areas the family should control. They may also fear that the more external exposure non-family executives get, the more likely the company is to lose them.

Unfortunately, this kind of sheltering deprives the non-family executives of personal-growth opportunities and a broader professional network, and it may hinder the development of stronger self-confidence and a sense of identity and self-worth. What's worse for the company is that as a result of lack of outside contact, employees have less to contribute

The mere fact that there is an independent board can play a role in attracting and retaining non-family executives — they will see the existence of such a board as further evidence that the family holds itself accountable, is open to input, will share information, and will think about things objectively.

to the company and less enthusiasm for their jobs. In other words, they are prevented from becoming as competent as a business owner would want them to be.

EXHIBIT 6 ▰▰▰▰▰▰▰▰▰▰▰▰▰▰▰▰▰▰▰▰▰▰

What Non-Family Executives Want

— Responsibility commensurate with their talent.

— A chance to make a difference in your company.

— A good relationship with your children.

— Fair treatment.

— Involvement in strategic planning and decision making.

— Information and open communication.

— To be heard.

— Recognition and praise.

— A relationship with the outside world.

Building a Foundation of Trust

As you can no doubt see, many of the factors that make non-family executives feel like a part of the team are profoundly based on trust. And while ultimately, trust must be mutual, the building of trust has to be initiated by the family and, most particularly, by the business leader.

One of the greatest impediments for the meaningful involvement of non-family executives in a family firm is the business leader's inability to trust others. And yet, the growth of a business is dependent on the extent to which the chief executive can delegate and can trust others.

If you're the business leader, take a moment to ask yourself, "Do I have the capacity to trust people?" If you happen to be the founder and you're like many entrepreneurs we know, the answer is probably, "Yes, but not easily."

Even though extending trust is difficult for you, it's something you can learn and something you can practice until it becomes more natural to you. Begin by being trustworthy yourself and by acting in a trusting manner toward others. Be consistent — do as you say you will do; avoid making exceptions or changing your mind just because you hold the power to do so. Be open. Let yourself be vulnerable. Be willing to share sensitive, but meaningful, business-oriented information (but don't burden non-family executives with your personal problems). Be willing to share power and authority and to delegate meaningful responsibilities.

Other ways to build trust are to be compassionate and to have empathy for others. It can be very hard for someone who has all the power, such as a business owner, to really understand what another person's life is like. It takes effort and sensitivity, and it takes getting outside of yourself to really pay attention to the other person's needs and circumstances. But the more you can do that, the more you can build trust with that person.

When you, the head of the business, exhibit trustworthiness yourself and extend trust to your non-family executives, you set an example for family members. You can reinforce their trust by making sure they know the non-family executives and by demonstrating how much faith you place in them. Sometimes a business owner might say, "If anything happens to me, you can count on Charlie." What he's telling you is how deeply he trusts Charlie.

When you act with trust, you inspire your non-family executives to trust in return and to be committed to the organization and the ownership. And you need this foundation of trust because you must be able to put some of your most precious assets into the hands of your senior non-family executives. You will depend on them to help mentor and develop your own children in the business. You will depend on them to watch after the business when you want to take a vacation or if you become ill. Because they're so exposed to so many parts of your life and they know how you relate to your spouse or how you treat your kids, you must also depend on them to be both understanding and discreet.

One of the greatest impediments for the meaningful involvement of non-family executives in a family firm is the business leader's inability to trust others And yet, the growth of a business is dependent on the extent to which the chief executive can delegate and can trust others.

26

Essentially, building trust with a non-family executive isn't any different than building trust with anybody else. It's just that sometimes family business owners find it more difficult to do the things that nourish trust. But we encourage you to try, because that foundation of trust will make all the difference in the world in your ability to attract and retain some of your most valuable employees — your non-family executives.

EXHIBIT 7

7 Ways To Build Trust

— Be consistent — do what you say you will do.

— Avoid making exceptions or changing your mind just because you have the power to do so.

— Let yourself be open and vulnerable.

— Share information and power.

— Be compassionate and show empathy.

— Extend trust to others.

— Let family members know how much you trust your non-family executives.

You'll go a long way toward making non-family executives a part of the team when you regard them, sincerely, as your equals. They're not the hired help. "If you believe that a non-family senior executive is something less than a peer," a Canadian family business leader once told a family business audience, "I suggest you will attract and retain people who fulfill your prophesy that they are less than capable of doing a good job."

Non-family employees want to develop and grow. Attracting and retaining the best people requires a family business to aggressively seek ways to give them new challenges, providing the motivation and potential non-financial rewards that make a job worth keeping even if greener grass might be available elsewhere.

An environment of trust and respect combined with an opportunity to grow and have ever more challenging and well-defined responsibility and authority will help persuade your most talented non-family executives that it is in their best interests to serve the best interests of your family business.

EXHIBIT 8

Best Practices For Managing Key Non-Family Executives

- Have a family employment policy and share it with your key non-family employees.

- Have a compensation policy that applies to all employees.

- Create a compensation system that helps non-family executives think, act and feel like owners.

- Share complete information with key non-family executives.

- Involve key non-family executives in strategic planning and decisions.

- Communicate clearly through actions, decisions and words the family business's mission, goals and values to and with non-family employees.

- Communicate family succession plans with key non-family executives.

V. *Managing The Transition To The Next Generation*

A man we'll call Roger and the family he works for represent almost the ideal when it comes to the relationship between a key non-family executive and a business-owning family. And the benefits of this good relationship are standing all parties in good stead now that the children are beginning to take positions of leadership in the family business.

Roger has been with The Bonner Co. for more than 18 years, and has seen it grow from being a miniature golf course to a conference center and resort that includes an elegant hotel, an 18-hole golf course, hiking trails and a dinner theater. When Roger started, he was assistant manager. Jerry and Martha Bonner, the husband and wife who founded the Southern California company, were impressed not only with his performance but also with the values that seemed to reflect their own — integrity, hard work, a demand for excellence, conscientiousness, empathy, and a respect for the bottom line. Jerry and Martha soon came to rely very heavily on Roger's talents. Their trust in him — and his in them — has grown deeper over the years, and Roger, as executive vice president, is essentially next-in-command after Jerry and Martha.

But Roger has always understood his position. The Bonners have three children — two sons and a daughter. They ranged in age from 9 to 16 when Roger joined the company. Now they are in their 20s and 30s. When Jerry and Martha first hired Roger, they didn't realize what an important role he might one day play in their company. But as they began to recognize the depth of his talent and to understand how valuable he would be to the growth of their company, they decided it was time for a talk.

Over dinner one evening, they told him how much they valued his contribution, and how much they hoped he would be with the company for a long, long time — and how much they hoped the company could do for him in return.

"But you've got so much ability and so much potential," said Jerry, "that we recognize that you might want to run your own company someday. And we can't promise you that that will happen here."

"You see, it's always been our dream that the children would come into the business and take over one day," added Martha.

Then Roger surprised the couple. He really didn't want to run his own business, he said. He liked playing a strong, supporting role. It suited his temperament, he said. He saw a lot of potential for the Bonners' business and looked forward to being a part of its growth.

"But I don't really need to be top dog," he said. "That's never been on my agenda."

In that and many conversations that followed, Roger and the Bonners talked about how Roger could help prepare the Bonner children for roles in the business. They agreed that while the children were teenagers and college students, Roger would find part-time and summer jobs for them in the company and that he would take on the responsibility of seeing that they got good, early work experience.

But the three of them also agreed that the children should not be pressured to come into the business. They had to *want* to join the business and be sure it was right for them. Roger also suggested that the Bonners begin to develop an employment policy that would govern the children's eventual entry into the business. "That way," Roger said, "the kids will understand that they have to meet certain expectations in order to earn the right to join."

With Roger's help, the Bonners crafted a policy that stipulated a college education (with preference given to an advanced degree) and successful employment outside the family business for a minimum of five years.

Then the Bonners did an unusual thing. Because they were so concerned about not putting pressure on their children to join the business and because they wanted the entry of the children to be as professional as possible, they made a request of Roger. "We want you to monitor the progress of each of the children, and when you think they're ready to come into the company and there's a job here for them, we want you to make the invitation," said Jerry. "We trust your judgment."

And that's the way it has worked. It took nearly 15 years, but now all three children hold responsible jobs in the company, and the oldest serves on the senior management team. The family laughs over the story of how Roger struck out the first time he invited one of the sons, Bryan, into the business. Bryan had just received a promotion at the hotel management company where he was working when Roger called him and said there was an opening in the family business and he and his parents would love to have Bryan consider it. "But I've just gotten this great new job! I can't leave now," Bryan said. A couple of years went by before another appropriate job opened up. Roger extended an invitation again, and this time, Bryan accepted.

One of Roger's most important responsibilities now — perhaps *the* most important responsibility — is the continued preparation of the children for higher and higher levels of leadership in the company. He has designed a program that exposes the younger Bonners to different parts of the operation in jobs that test their abilities, gauge their interest, and provide them with valuable experience.

Roger is about seven years younger than Jerry and Martha, but he's not particularly concerned about what will happen when the couple retires and the kids take over. Ever since he joined the company, the parents have demonstrated their respect for Roger and made sure the kids knew how important Roger was to the company. Roger's friendly, low-key personality — and his intelligence — won the kids over early and they have an easy relationship with him to this day.

Roger would admit that there are several other reasons he's not worried about the kids taking over. For one thing, they're all bright and have good ideas, and they get along pretty well with one another. Roger thinks they might be fun to work for. "And even though Jerry and Martha hired me, my commitment is not just to them," says Roger. "I feel loyalty to the whole family and I really love the business. In fact, I've been so committed to this business that when I think any family member is making a wrong decision, I don't hesitate to say so — respectfully, of course. I think everyone in the family knows that I have the business's interests at heart."

Another reason Roger's not worried about the kids taking over? If he wanted to, Roger could retire tomorrow. Money is not a problem. Jerry and Martha have seen to it that Roger, their most-valued non-family executive, has been amply rewarded for the contribution he has made to the growth of their company and Roger is today a wealthy man.

We recognize that few business-owning families and non-family executives are as fortunate as the people in the case of the Bonner business — where roles are clearly understood and people are happy to play them. We also know that giving a valued lieutenant like Roger the responsibility of inviting the children into the business is not for everyone.

But a lot can be learned from Jerry, Martha and Roger about the role a non-family executive can play in the development of the children in the business and in the gradual, graceful transition of the business to new leadership. They make it look easy but, as most business owners know, it's not.

Setting the Stage for Succession

One of the major advantages of hiring non-family executives is that they can mentor your children and help prepare them for leadership roles in your business. This helps minimize or eliminate the emotional pressure that builds up when Mom or Dad are mentoring or supervising the children directly — much in the same way that it's better to have a trained instructor teach your children to drive a car than teach them

31

yourself. The non-family executive can give the young person valuable, objective feedback that parents might be hesitant to provide or too emotional in the way they provide it.

In fact, we urge top-level family leaders to be very clear with non-family managers about what's expected as they supervise younger family members. Non-family managers will have a natural tendency to go easy on family subordinates, reasoning that "someday, this kid is going to be my boss, and if I say something that's not nice to him, he may remember it and do me harm sometime in the future." But young family members need honest feedback about their performance and need to know what they must do to measure up if they want to move up the leadership ladder.

One of the major advantages of hiring non-family executives is that they can mentor your children and help prepare them for leadership roles in your business.

There should be a clear understanding by all — family executives, non-family executives, and younger family members — that straightforward feedback is expected and is a part of the training and mentoring process.

As non-family executives guide the development of your sons and daughters in the business, they are in fact setting the stage for the eventual succession process that will see your children take over leadership positions in the company and, finally, the company itself.

As time goes on, non-family executives may actually participate in the succession planning process. Or, in cases where founders are dragging their feet about doing succession and estate planning, non-family executives that are especially close to them — a CFO, for example — may even trigger the process.

These are valid — and valuable — roles for non-family executives to play. Still, they need to be played thoughtfully and with care, and both sides — the business owner and the non-family manager — need to understand the role that the non-family manager has undertaken and to be clear on expectations each has for the other in the process.

When non-family executives catalyze succession, wise business owners will try to determine whether they are a constructive voice of reason, prodding reticent family members to do necessary financial, organizational, strategic, and succession planning. Or are they the loyal, long-time, trusted retainers of the senior generation executives, reinforcing fears and a status quo consistent with their own needs and agendas?

Involving non-family executives in the succession process must be done with wisdom and care. There are some limitations that should be respected, and there are processes or structures you can create that will make the transition to the next generation go more smoothly. We offer these suggestions and cautions:

Discourage non-family executives from being a mentor to one individual for too long. Research suggests that sometime between three and five years, "students" begin to discover their mentors' weaknesses and to turn on them. This is a natural occurrence and no one is at fault. Expose your sons and daughters to a variety of mentors over time so they encounter new perspectives and a diversity of good role models.

Use your outside directors — not your non-family executives — for succession selection. Despite the success of the Bonner family in using Roger to develop and bring the children into the business, Roger has not been asked to recommend a successor. Nor, in our opinion, should he be. That puts him, as an employee, in a very awkward spot. Independent directors are in a better position to evaluate and offer input about potential CEO successors. They have nothing to risk and can be more objective.

Develop a succession or transition task force. This can be an excellent tool, whether or not you have an outside board. Such a task force would be made up of a team of non-candidates for succession, such as: An independent director, two key non-family managers, a professional advisor or consultant, and two key family members. **Their purpose is to serve as a transition device, *not* to choose the successor.** They may identify the issues of transition in a particular company and ways to preserve the company culture during the transition. They may even establish the process of transition, help define how the choice of a successor is made, and anticipate the side effects of transition.

It is their job to raise succession questions and build a proper level of awareness in the organization. They don't focus on "who?" and "when?" Instead, they concentrate on "what?" and "how will it affect the organization?" A good succession task force asks questions like, "How do we communicate this to the organization? Is the organization prepared for this and sensitive to it? How does this affect the careers of others?" **When a succession task force does its job well, the transition can be culturally compatible and considerate of the whole organization, not just the successor and the incumbent.**

Once succession plans are known, communicate them to all non-

family key executives. Knowing your plans keeps them from feeling excluded. Because it keeps people from guessing, it limits the possibilities that there will be people taking sides, developing allies, and playing politics. Further, it gives them a chance to contribute to the eventual successor's growth and development. And finally, sharing succession plans and management development plans is a real trust builder because it is a generous thing to do, and, in a way, is almost an intimate thing to do.

The period of transition from one generation to the next is a time of great uncertainty for non-family executives. They are going from the known to the unknown, from a system they understand to one they don't.

Walk in the Non-Family Executive's Shoes

The period of transition from one generation to the next is a time of great uncertainty for non-family executives. They are going from the known to the unknown, from a system they understand to one they don't. They are keenly aware of the possibility that Junior might bring in his own team. Running through their minds are such questions as: Will I still have a job? (Usually, but not always.) Are the rules of the game going to be the same? (Probably not.) Will my role change? (Probably so.) They may even be concerned about the job security and roles of other people they value in the company.

Any number of things can induce insecurity in a non-family executive during transition. If an older non-family executive has given enormous loyalty to the incumbent CEO, he knows that the successor will wonder if he can transfer his loyalty to the new leadership. There may have been some rivalry between the non-family executive and the newly appointed successor. Or, a non-family executive may have given the younger generation honest but uncomplimentary feedback in the past and may worry now that the new successor is harboring a grudge.

Under such uncertainty, it's not uncommon for non-family managers to begin to exhibit unusual behavior. For the first time, they may ask for an employment contract or express a desire for ownership and hint that they might leave if they don't get what they want. A stunned business owner may react in the worst way, questioning an executive's loyalty, and saying,"How could you do this to me just when I need you most?"

It will be helpful for all concerned if the family is sensitive to these fears, anticipates anxiety on the part of the non-family managers, and takes action to minimize uncertainty. One of the ways to do so is to establish the succession or transition task force suggested above.

It's also advisable for the incumbent CEO and the successor to be talking with each other and coming to decisions together about the future of the non-family key executives who have been such an important part of Mom or Dad's team. We've seen cases where Dad doesn't trust the successor and wants to protect his own top non-family executive. So before the successor takes over, Dad offers the favorite executive a "pot of gold" — say, a financial incentive to stick around another five years. This imposes on the successor an executive he may not want and makes it clear that Dad doesn't have confidence in him. Far better for Dad to explain the role of each non-family executive and how he or she fits into the overall picture, and let the successor say, "I really want to keep Frances on as COO. I know she's feeling very uncertain about the future. Maybe it's time we offered her some incentive to stay on another five years."

At a time of transition, the incumbent and successors may want to give serious consideration to the possibility of offering employment contracts and other incentives, even though the company has not offered them before. But the members of the succeeding generation need to be involved in such decisions because it is they who will incur the burden as well as, it is hoped, the benefits.

The Ambitious Non-Family Executive

What if one of your non-family executives wants to be the next CEO? **If the members of the next generation don't appear to have what it takes to be the top leader, then a competent non-family executive is a good insurance policy to have.** However, if one or more young family members are of CEO caliber, you must make it clear to the non-family executive that you intend for succession to stay within the family but that he or she will play a very central and very important role in your company.

Some form of "golden handcuffs" will probably be in order. You might say, very openly, "My son and daughter are going to be leading this company and we're satisfied that we're keeping leadership in family hands for the right reasons. You have great talent and we value you tremendously, and we want you as a key part of the team. What is it going to take to keep you here?" Together, you can look at it as a problem-solving situation. You might be asked to offer phantom stock, or perhaps the non-family executive will be happy to head a division of your company.

If the non-family executive has an overwhelming drive to be CEO, you have to face the fact that sooner or later, he or she will be leaving your business. If that's the case, **you need to make sure your company has some management depth and is not overly-dependent on one person.**

Cleaning House

It's an unfortunate situation when all the key non-family executives are roughly the same age as the retiring CEO and they're all retiring at about the same time. It means a great loss of corporate memory and years of experience, and it can be dangerous to a company.

If you have planned well enough and long enough ahead, however, you won't find yourself in this situation. You will have staggered the ages of the non-family executives you hire and you will have deliberately hired some very young, talented people who can be developed over a long period of time. When the successor takes over, he or she will then have a healthy combination of older, seasoned executives and somewhat younger, experienced managers who are ready to take on senior-level challenges.

Not every non-family executive will survive the transition. In fact, a transition period can offer a good opportunity for some needed house cleaning. Some non-family executives will leave voluntarily. The decision whether others stay or go will have to be made on their competence and a range of other factors. **The important thing is that it not be left to the successor to do the "dirty work." You don't want your son or daughter to be saddled with a reputation as someone who chops off heads.** That's not good for the successor or the family, and it's certainly not good for the morale of the company.

Cleaning house can be done gracefully and humanely, and it needs to be done by the incumbents before they leave.

VI. *The Non-Family CEO*

Despite a family's strong desire to keep top leadership of its business in the family, it is sometimes necessary to select a chief executive officer from outside of the family. Perhaps an incumbent CEO has died unexpectedly and next-generation family members are too young and inexperienced for the role. Or perhaps an incumbent CEO wishes to retire and no one in the next generation wants the job — or no one in the next generation is competent enough to handle it. Or perhaps the company is in serious difficulty and recognizes the need to hire someone who can turn it around. By the time he reached his late 40s, one owner had been running his family's company for nearly 20 years. He felt he was stagnating and that the business could benefit from fresh leadership, but there was no one from within the family yet to provide it. In other cases, CEOs just want to exit early to pursue other interests.

These are all good reasons to turn to a competent outsider to run the business — at least until qualified family members are available once again.

Some families may think that if there is not a son or daughter to take over, the business will have to be sold. Many now recognize that it's not the end of a family firm if you bring in a non-family leader. More and more, we are seeing families turn to non-family leadership as interim or "bridge" or "buffer" CEOs when members of the younger generation are too young to assume leadership and the senior generation wants to retire but to hold on to ownership.

Sometimes the heirs themselves, thrown into leadership positions prematurely, hire someone to, in effect, be the bridge CEO. Henry Ford II became head of Ford Motor Company at the age of 28 after Edsel Ford died unexpectedly at an early age. He brought in Ernest Beech as his mentor and, he acknowledged, as a bridge CEO until he himself had gained enough knowledge and experience to take charge. In later years, Henry II said that Beech "was really the chief, and I was watching and learning, hopefully. He knew a lot more than I did and so the major operating decisions, he made them."

> *More and more, we are seeing families turn to non-family leadership as interim or "bridge" or "buffer" CEOs.*

After he became the non-family CEO of Haviland Enterprises, Inc., a family-owned chemical distribution business in Grand Rapids, MI, in 1991, H. Richard "Dick" Garner pulled the company out of difficult straits. He believes other family businesses could benefit from hiring a non-family CEO, provided the family is willing to surrender some control.

"The first and most critical requirement is that the company be truly ready for some change," says Garner. "Or, does the family just want someone else to continue to do the things that they've done forever and ever and look over their shoulders? That would not work. The CEO must have clear authority to manage the business if he wants to move in and be the true CEO."

Ideally, your non-family CEO would be someone you could promote from within — an executive with five or more years of experience in your company. But as many business-owning families have learned, you can go outside the company and still have a successful experience.

Garner, other non-family CEOs, and some business leaders who have been through the process offer these suggestions to business families considering an outside CEO:

— Be sure all key players agree. Everybody in his family went along with the decision to hire an outsider, says a business leader who felt he was stagnating. In another family, when the 66-year-old founder and his family brought in a non-family CEO, the 34-year-old son, who was president and COO, said, "The whole senior management team is very excited. When [the non-family CEO] came into the picture, I realized that all this is going to do is make me a better CEO. Sure, my ego can come in and say this doesn't feel good. But once you put that ego aside, you can see another whole world." And when the newcomer accepted the position, the founder's wife said, "Thank you for helping my family."

— Look for a good fit. "Make sure the CEO has a personality compatible with the key people from the family in the business, and maybe even those who aren't in the business," says Dick Garner. "It's a unique situation. It's nothing whatsoever like running a public company."

You will want a CEO whose vision and strategy for the business match those of your family. You will also want someone who will have credibility not just in the business but also in the family — the family members who are not directly involved in the business should feel that the CEO is someone they can trust.

— Look for someone who can train a successor. Make it clear that one of the CEO's most important responsibilities will be to train the next CEO, whether or not that person is a family member. Like other senior executives, the CEO should have the ability to coach and mentor younger people in the business, including family members.

— Prepare your children and your employees for the new CEO.
One business-owning couple turned to a trusted attorney for help. "He contacted each one of our children personally and discussed with them what our thoughts were and what we were attempting to do and got their thoughts on the subject," said the wife.

Family members who are not directly involved in the business should feel that the CEO is someone they can trust.

You also need to explain to employees why you're going outside the family for a CEO. Longtime employees especially may feel that a non-family chief executive is a threat to them and to their relationship with the family. If the owners adequately communicate their decision to the employees and show 100-percent support for the new CEO, the employees should grow more comfortable with the change.

— Once you've hired a non-family CEO, let go of control. Otherwise, the transition won't work. If you're a business owner who is still working day-to-day in the company, you may have to take conscious steps not to undermine the non-family CEO and to make it clear that he or she is now in charge. This may mean not letting employees bypass the CEO and come to you with problems, the way they used to. You may have to remind them of the proper chain of authority.

— Keep communicating. The family needs to share complete information with the CEO — including "family secrets." Does a family employee have an alcohol problem that affects her performance, for example? In turn, the family should expect that the CEO will keep it fully informed, with frequent updates on the company's successes, challenges, and plans.

Having to go outside the family for a CEO obviously isn't the end of the world for a family business. It may take some getting used to, but when it's done well, the business prospers, the family prospers, and, in time, leadership returns to a new generation of family members who have been well-trained by the company's "bridge" CEO.

VII. *Just Rewards: Compensation And Incentives For Non-family Executives*

When it comes to rewarding non-family executives, family business owners face several challenges: How, for example, can you structure compensation so that it links the performance of an executive to the long-term performance of your company? How can you avoid overpaying in your effort to retain valuable talent, while at the same time being sure you're providing sufficient compensation to keep non-family managers happy and motivated?

Obviously you will gather information on market rates for key positions from your industry associations and professional advisors. And that's a good place to start. But when you are dealing with all the issues that surround non-family executives in family firms, there are many more considerations than just market rates. What do you want your compensation strategy to achieve, for example? What if someone with a lot to offer your company wants stock ownership as part of the deal? How should pay for non-family executives compare with pay for executives who are family members?

In designing compensation and incentives for non-family executives, family firms often seek three objectives: (1) To align executive and owner goals; (2) To retain excellent executives for the long term; and (3) To assure executives that their careers are secure.

It's helpful to consider the situation of the non-family executive. If it's a policy — or a reality — that only family members can hold the position of CEO in your company, for example, then the non-family executive's ability to ascend to the top is thwarted. Some business owners believe that less opportunity should equal more pay for non-family managers on whom they know they can depend.

Family business owners need to keep in mind that they

In designing compensation and incentives for non-family executives, family firms often seek three objectives: (1) To align executive and owner goals; (2) To retain excellent executives for the long term; and (3) To assure executives that their careers are secure.

41

must compete in the marketplace for the value of the services of non-family executives. Furthermore, excellent non-family executives would have opportunities for creating personal wealth in other situations, such as with stock options in internet startups or in large corporations. The question a business-owning family needs to ask itself, then, is, "How do we put our excellent non-family executives into a position where they have an opportunity to become wealthy, over and above their annual salary?"

We think the best way to reward your most-valued non-family executives is through a package that combines a salary that is market-based (as should be the salaries of family executives) and incentives that give them a long-term perspective. Annual bonuses may not be the best choice in a family business because they nurture a one-year perspective rather than the longer view so necessary to family firms.

Family business owners need to keep in mind that they must compete in the marketplace for the value of the services of non-family executives.

Here are some of the ways family firms try to meet their objectives through incentives:

Stock Ownership

It's tempting to lure talented executives to a family business with hints or outright promises that they may get some equity in the company. But providing stock ownership is not usually the wisest way to reward non-family executives. **We advise business owners never to suggest or promise that there will be stock ownership in an executive's future.** Such hints and promises can come back to haunt owners who change their minds.

To be sure, awarding stock ownership does have some benefits. Besides making a position in your company financially attractive, it tends to make key managers more conscious of the long-term perspective. What's more, giving stock doesn't require cash and, at least in the short run, may seem cheaper to the business owner.

Only about 3 to 5 percent of family businesses offer stock to employees, however. Most business-owning families, are reluctant or unwilling to give real ownership to real people outside the family. They don't want to dilute family ownership, nor do they want the increased employee scrutiny of family actions that stock ownership would invite. And because they don't want ex-employees owning stock, they must buy back the stock when an employee leaves or is terminated, which can put a cash strain on the company. Sharing ownership also presents legal and administrative complications, including the need to put a value on the stock. In addition, as many family business advisors point out, offering equity to non-family executives can change the political flavor of a company and adds a "wild card" to an ownership mix that may already be confused and diverse.

EXHIBIT 9 ▋▋▋▋▋▋▋▋▋▋▋▋▋▋▋▋▋▋▋▋▋▋▋▋

Share Of Compensation Typically Received In Incentives

Management Level	Performance		
	Outstanding	**Good**	**Below Average**
Top managers	50% - 75%	20% - 50%	0% - 20%
Middle to upper-middle managers	20% - 50%	10% - 30%	0 % - 10%
Lower-middle to middle managers	20% - 30%	10% - 20%	0% - 10%

Reprinted from *Family Business Compensation*, No. 5 in the Family Business Leadership Series.

We find that offering equity works best if the business is already publicly traded, or is quasi-publicly traded in that the company has already given ownership to a number of employees or if there are outside venture partners.

Often stock is shared for the wrong reasons, when other vehicles or just good management would satisfy employees' needs. It's helpful to examine why key executives want stock ownership. Financial reward is one reason — key employees may wish to build their personal wealth or share in the company's growth in value. Later, we suggest some alternatives for helping non-family members achieve financial growth without participating in ownership.

Some key managers may want stock ownership as a way of providing for future security, but an employment contract or retirement plan may be more appropriate in meeting that need.

Some employees want the prestige of being an owner, a partner, or a principal. And sometimes, employees find that such prestige enables them to be more effective on behalf of the company. However, titles can be designed to convey the same meaning — for example, "partner" could mean partner in profits rather than partner in equity.

Key managers may desire stock ownership for reasons of personal pride. They may see it as a symbol of special recognition from owners, or as a reward for long and loyal service. But owners can confer recognition by bestowing important titles, publicly praising employees, or developing special personal relationships with them.

Some employees see stock ownership as a sign of the owners' trust and commitment. They may hope that having stock will provide them access to "inside" information usually reserved for owners or give them an opportunity to participate in key decisions. Such desires may signal that the business owner is being too secretive, which may result in harming employee performance or hindering the building of trust. In such cases, the business owner can try to be more open with non-family executives, share more information with them, and involve them in decision making.

Still, some family business owners are comfortable with giving stock. One family set aside 20 percent of the stock of their company for its management team. The board of directors put the company's non-family CEO in charge of a committee to decide how to distribute the set-aside shares. "He decides how much he feels he should have for himself and then what he needs to attract other good team players to work with him," says a company owner.

Other Options

We have seen many families successfully choose one of several options other than stock ownership — options that neatly tie wealth-building incentives to performance and other objectives.

— **"Pot of Gold."** This is our terminology for an incentive that says, "Stick with me long enough and I'll give you a big, pleasant surprise." More specifically, a business owner might offer a lump sum: "If you're here with me for 10 years, I'm going to give you a $1 million bonus." But it could take other forms as well, such as a lifetime annuity if an executive stays until she's 62 years old. Or it might be offered in phantom stock (described below). A pot of gold offers a business owner a chance to do something special for an individual, valued executive. It's not something owners do often.

— Long-term bonuses. These are generally available to many or all of your executives and are linked to company performance. They tie an executive to the company longer and encourage a longer-term view. The bonus may, for example, be a percentage of operating profits — or book value growth – over a three-to-five period. Earned bonuses are then vested and paid out over the next three-to-five years, contingent on continued employment with the company (with special arrangements in case of death, disability or sale of the business). Such programs motivate both performance and long-term employment.

— Phantom/shadow stock. This is a much talked about but seldom practiced idea. Only about three percent of family businesses offer phantom stock to non-family employees. "Phantom" or "shadow" stock is an equity substitute that behaves like real stock without conferring rights of ownership. It serves as a longer-term cash bonus plan tied to the company's performance as if it were stock, and can encourage employees to think about the business's long-term goals. Under conditions set forth in the plan, the business buys back the phantom shares with cash; some plans vest only after a certain period of time, as a means of retaining the employee. Under some plans, the value of dividends paid to actual shareholders are also paid to phantom owners.

Many business-owning families resist offering phantom stock because, as with real stock, it's difficult to put a value on the shares in a private company. Some families also fear that setting a price will create family expectations and estate-planning precedents. For example, suppose a non-family executive retires and cashes in his shares at a price that was probably set by the CEO, with the consent of the board. If family members think the price is low, they may worry that the company is not doing well. Or, if an appraiser is brought in to evaluate the phantom shares and the price he comes up with becomes known to family members, they may start making estate plans based on that price. But it's an artificial price determined only for the non-family executives, a fact that needs to be made very clear to family members.

— Equity in another of the business-owning family's investments. Under this option, the non-family executive reaps benefits from new ventures the family is starting up but intends to sell eventually, or from investments that the family makes. For example, the family might decide to invest in someone else's entrepreneurial company. It could then tell the non-family executive, "Joe, we've bought a 20-percent stake in Widget-Tech and we're setting aside 5 percent for you. When we sell, that's for you." This is a great way to show appreciation to a non-family executive for all that she or he has contributed to the family's company. The risk, of course, is that the side venture or investment loses money instead of making a profit. But it's the family's money, not the employee's, that's at risk

Exhibit 10 ▮

Some Bonus Incentive Examples

■ **Company A** believes the current year's profit levels are about normal. Any profit next year that exceeds this year's level will be shared with management. Twenty percent of the profit increase will be evenly divided among the top five managers. Ten percent of the profit gain will be evenly divided among the next 12 managers.

■ **Company B** has decided that its minimum pre-tax return on capital should be 15 percent, assuring shareholders of a reasonable return on their investment. One-third of the profits beyond that minimum return-on-capital threshold are placed in a pool to be distributed among executives. Half of these pooled profits are shared proportionate to executives' salaries — thereby rewarding team accomplishment. The other half is distributed at the discretion of the CEO, based upon each individual's achievements during the year.

■ **Company C** seeks to reward sales growth and customer satisfaction. Each executive gets a bonus based on a percentage of salary equal to the percentage increase in the company's total revenues that year. Each also receives $5,000 in additional bonus payments for each 10 percent reduction in customer returns or allowances.

■ **Company D** bases its formula on total dollar profit improvement over three years and pays out one-third of the earned bonus each year, always retaining two-thirds for the future.

Reprinted from *Family Business Compensation,* No. 5 in the Family Business Leadership Series.

Sometimes, in a misguided attempt to reward a valued non-family executive, a family will say, "Here's a deal for you. We found this great venture and the family is going to buy 20 percent of it. If you're interested, you can *buy* in with us." This puts the employee in an awkward position — he may not want to put what he considers a significant amount of his personal savings into an investment that's tied to the family that he works with and that his job depends on. He may also be concerned that if he doesn't invest, the family will think he doesn't trust them. On the other hand, he hasn't got the time to investigate the proposed investment himself because he's spending all his time working for the family.

This is also awkward for the family. Suppose the investment doesn't work out. The family's 20-percent stake may be just a drop in the bucket in terms of its total wealth, but the 2-percent or 5-percent lost by the employee may represent a very substantial chunk of his wealth or his income.

It's better by far for the family to give pieces of side ventures and investments as gifts to prized executives. The family can say, "We've valued the gift as best we can as if we were giving stock options in our company. We want you to achieve the same kind of wealth that you would have achieved if you did have stock." This way, the family avoids compromising non-family executives and stands a much better chance of motivating them and making them feel rewarded and appreciated — all factors in retaining them.

Can You Be Too Generous?

Years ago, in a column we wrote for a business magazine, we told the story of Pete, a well-intentioned, family business owner who backed himself into a corner over an employee pension plan. His paternalism and feelings of guilt over exploiting employees during the early, tough years of his business left him wide open to accepting his accountant's suggestion to set up a pension program based on a profit-sharing plan. The clincher: Pete could shelter 15 percent of his own pay if he put aside an equivalent percentage for all other employees.

Pete's accountant also made another good point: The plan was discretionary. If business was bad, there was no commitment to contribute. But Pete failed to establish a formula for tying the amount of the contribution to company profits so that in good years employees would get the maximum contribution but in bad years they would get less. In fact, avoiding taxes motivated Pete more than providing an incentive for employees to be more profit-conscious. What's more, Pete was secretive. Information about profits was never shared. If profits were down, he reasoned, wouldn't good employees leave?

Exhibit 11 ▐██

Incentives For Key
Non-Family Executives

Concept	Advantages	Disadvantages
Discretionary Bonus	*Encourages clear goal-setting and comprehensive review	*Rarely done well; usually uncomfortable for both parties
Discretionary Perquisites	*Strengthens personal-family ties	*Others may be offended; can create paternalism
Annual Profit Bonus	*Related to ability, to pay and to profits	*Not long-term oriented; company performance can be affected by uncontrollable events
Long-Range or Multi-Year Profit Bonus	*Ties employee to company longer; encourages more important long-term view	*Profits don't necessarily measure most criteria (i.e., return on equity, market share, etc.)
Phantom Stock	*Long-term orientation and related to shareholder benefit	*Difficult to value for private company
Real Common Stock	*Long-term orientation and related to shareholder benefit. Confers greater emotional meaning or status.	*Complicated legal administration and difficult to value
Non-Company Investment Opportunities	*Strengthens personal-family ties. Doesn't affect company's stock ownership.	*Not readily available. Any failure brings major disappointment.

Reprinted from *Family Business Compensation*, No.5 in the Family Business Leadership Series.

Over time, even when business was off, Pete continued to make maximum contributions to the plan. "After all that these people have done over the difficult years, how can you cut their pension?" he asked. The 15-percent profit-sharing contribution became a permanent benefit.

As the years went by, Pete came to feel burdened by the high cost of the pension plan and wished it had been tied to actual profits. But he was still unwilling to share numbers with his employees and he feared that cutting the contribution would hurt morale.

While this story surrounds a compensation issue that applies to an owner's relationship with all employees, its importance is magnified when it comes to compensating key non-family employees. They need information about the company's numbers, not only to perform more effectively on behalf of the company but also to understand how their compensation and incentives relate to company performance at any given time. Information motivates all employees — and especially key employees — as they understand company performance and how they contribute to and benefit from it.

This story says something else to us. Every decision you make about compensating non-family executives will have some consequences. And no plan is perfect. But whatever you consider doing to reward your key players, think through all the angles and potential consequences as thoroughly as you can so that you can avoid or minimize adverse effects. What, for example, are your motives for offering a certain type of compensation (and the motives for key executives in desiring it)? How will succumbing to those motivations affect the outcomes? Can needs on both sides be met more appropriately in some other way? Pete, as we see, fell into a trap because he was overly motivated by a desire for tax savings and by his paternalism.

As we said in an earlier chapter, we encourage family businesses to adopt compensation policies that apply to both family and non-family employees and executives. Such policies and other compensation issues are discussed in more detail in *Family Business Compensation,* booklet No. 5 in the Family Business Leadership Series.

Ultimately, family businesses have to find ways to compensate and reward non-family executives so that they don't leave for financial reasons. As you plan your compensation strategy, however,

A non-family candidate for an executive position is "apt to be looking for other than money, because if he's good, he can get money anywhere."

take heart in the knowledge that **compensation is just one aspect of your relationship with non-family managers. They're not in it just for the money. While they expect to be compensated fairly, other factors count for much as well: responsibility, the opportunity to make a difference in a company, the ability to participate in major decisions, respect, recognition, and time off to watch a little daughter or son play in a soccer match.**

As one business owner told us, a non-family candidate for an executive position is "apt to be looking for other than money, because if he's good, he can get money anywhere."

VIII. *An Open Letter To The Non-family Executive*

If you're a new non-family executive in a family company, or if you're thinking about accepting a management position in a family firm, you may be wondering how to make the experience a successful one. It's a wise thing to think about, because family firms pose many challenges to executives that they don't encounter in other companies.

Based on our years of experience working with hundreds of family-owned businesses, we offer the following observations:

—The opportunity for ownership is probably not on the table. Only about 3 percent of family businesses in this country give equity to non-family managers. There are some solid reasons why it's not a good idea for family firms to offer equity. Doing so dilutes the family's ownership and, over time, can dilute its control. Families recognize that someday, stock has to be bought back, and often, this can come at the wrong time and put a strain on the business. It's also difficult to decide who should and who should not receive equity in a company. So, even if the CEO hints that you might have ownership one day, don't take it too seriously.

However, as a key non-family executive, you should expect to be well-rewarded — with a fair market-rate salary and incentives that might include phantom stock, bonuses, or other financial considerations.

— Becoming CEO may not be in the picture. While we urge family businesses to create career paths for non-family executives that enable them to aspire to the highest levels in a company, the dream of many — if not most — business owners is to pass leadership of the company on to their children. Before you are hired, the owners should make it clear whether or not the CEO role or other top positions are reserved for family. Armed with that information, you can make a more intelligent decision about whether or not a given family company is right for you. Keep in mind, however, that the CEO's job is not the only important position in the company. If your temperament and ego permit, you might find some other senior-level role equally or even more satisfying.

— All family businesses have "family issues." These range from who in the family is permitted to join the business to how sibling rivalry affects other employees and the business itself. They can include what happens when the owner's son-in-law, a high-level executive in the company, gets a divorce from the owner's daughter, or when the founder and his children cannot agree on the direction of the company, or there's a desire on the part of an owner to have the company provide employment for Cousin Tammy, who just can't seem to keep a job elsewhere. **You need to anticipate that family relationships will affect the business and that the business in turn will affect the family.** We offer a few specific suggestions for skirting the minefields of family issues below, but we urge you now to educate yourself about the way family businesses work. The fact that you are reading the booklet is an auspicious start and suggests that you want to be successful in your role as a non-family manager. Many colleges and universities around the country have family business programs that offer seminars for family business owners and key employees. A number of books and publications are also available to assist you. For information on several, please visit our website at www.fbop.com.

Be loyal to the business, not to any one member of the family or part of the family.

— **You will never really be "part of the family."** No matter how well you are treated, no matter how much the family likes you, and no matter how many family events you are invited to, you are not a member of the family.

You may be the only non-family employee invited to a family wedding. It's likely the owner will confide in you, and you will be exposed to personal information about the family. But don't mislead yourself — you still aren't part of the family.

It's best to be as professional as you possibly can. Be friendly and polite, but keep a little distance. Don't let a desire for special treatment by the family become part of your emotional need. With the family, family will always come first. Family relationships are stronger than other relationships.

Enhance Your Chances For Success

Having made these four observations, we offer these specific suggestions for enhancing your chances of success as a non-family executive in a family business:

—**Understand that there's no substitute for competence.** Competence will get you through tough times and will help you survive a transition to the next generation. It's your competence that will win the respect and loyalty of the company's family leaders. Keep investing in your personal development. (But keep your personal network of contacts alive. While competence is your best security, there are no guarantees that any job will last forever.)

— Make the business your constituency. Be loyal to the business, not to any one member of the family or part of the family. You were hired by the business. Focus on what is best for the business and consistently represent that point of view. In that way, you serve the whole family.

— Lead the business to the next level of professionalism. This is especially important if you are among the first non-family executives a business owner has hired. The need for professionalism may not be one that an owner can articulate. More likely, you've been hired to address a particular problem — like sales, or marketing, or finance. But now you have a remarkable opportunity to help a business move from being entrepreneurial to being a company that plans for strategic growth, puts needed policies in place, emphasizes team decision making, and hires and promotes on a merit basis (family members included!). From this vantage point, you can also promote the idea of putting an independent board in place, if the company doesn't have one. The establishment of such a board will advance the company's professionalism even further.

— Take your role as a teacher seriously. The more a family relies on you as a valued, non-family executive, the more it will expect you to mentor and help develop the younger family members for management and leadership roles. Consider this responsibility a given, and remember that the owners' children are their most treasured assets.

— Avoid becoming entangled in family disputes. It's not your job to be the mediator or referee. Avoid triangles — where one family member criticizes another to you or wants you carry messages ("Tell my brother that. . ."). Help get communication going between the two people, but don't become a conduit yourself. Non-family managers often serve as go-betweens because they think they're doing a favor and contributing. But they're not.

— Don't take personal responsibility for what you can't control. In an effort to be helpful, a non-family manager may try to solve a problem when family members are disagreeing. Unless there is agreement, their positions can change, unpredictably, at any time. In a situation like this, make a recommendation to the owners and let them take the responsibility. Remember that you don't have the final say.

— Emphasize the notion of "team." Sometimes an executive feels more secure if he or she is the most favored non-family manager. Business owners tend to manage and meet with people one at a time — that way, they can shield themselves from the power of consensus. But this approach encourages individuals to seek the status of "No. 1 Advisor."

Almost always, this backfires. We urge non-family managers to promote executive team meetings to share information and alternatives. And always think of yourself as an equal member of the team — not a member more equal than others.

— Support the succession process, don't block it. Avoid taking sides as to who gets chosen. Be patient — the process will have many ups and downs and, especially frustrating, backs and forths. Champion and cheer the successor's success. It's likely that the incumbent and the successor will complain about each other. Listen with heart, but don't take sides.

— Be cautious about being a confidant. You may feel privileged to learn private family information, but it's more prudent to keep the relationship strictly professional.

— Be wary about asking for an employment contract. Many non-family executives have the perception that family businesses are capricious and that owners may make a decision to fire someone out of their own temperament or emotionalism. When that is their perception, non-family executives often say, "I'll never work for a family business unless they give me an employment contract."

Some family business owners have no problem with being asked for an employment contract. But a lot of business owners resist employment contracts. Their attitude is, "That's a self-interested, un-trusting way to approach a job." So, if you want to ask for an employment contract, recognize that you might get a negative reaction.

Some families will offer an employment contract as a vote of confidence, but in our view, it has to be genuinely offered, not demanded. It's probably safe to ask for an employment contract if such contracts represent standard practice in your industry or if a particular business has operated with employment contracts for many years. In most cases, however, if you feel you need a contract, you probably don't want to work for the company you're considering.

— Work hard to earn trust. In a family business, this can be difficult — first, because you are the outsider, and, second, because business owners, especially founders, often lack the ability to trust. As we counsel business owners in Chapter IV, you begin to build trust by being trustworthy yourself and by offering trust. Think of trust as a two-way street. If it's hard for the owner of the business you work for to be trusting, take the first step.

EXHIBIT 12 ■■■■■■■■■■■■■■■■■■■■■■■■■■■■■■■■■■■■■■

10 Steps to Success As A
Non-Family Business Executive

— Be competent.

— Regard the business as your constituency.

— Help professionalize the business.

— Take your role as a teacher seriously.

— Don't get involved in family disputes.

— Avoid Triangles.

— Emphasize teamwork and be a part of the team.

— Support the succession process.

— Listen with heart, but don't take sides in family conflicts.

— Work hard to earn trust.

— Don't threaten family control or family unity. At Ingram Industries, a Nashville-based multibillion-dollar industry, Chip Lacy built up his subsidiary, Ingram Micro, from next to nothing to an $8 billion computer wholesaler, the largest in the world. By the mid 1990s, he wanted to take Ingram Micro public. According to *Fortune* magazine, Lacy wanted complete autonomy and he pressured Ingram Industries chairman Martha Ingram to put her and her four children's shares of Ingram Micro into a trust to be voted by the management. To the shock of the computer distribution industry, Martha Ingram wouldn't budge and Lacy resigned.

It's not your job to be the mediator or referee. Avoid triangles — where one family member criticizes another to you or wants you carry messages.

Successful, seasoned non-family executives often counsel younger non-family managers to be part of the solution, not part of the problem. For example, if a family member is not yet prepared to take over a company but Dad clearly wants him to, don't jockey for position — take a leader-ship role in helping the son develop his potential instead.

— **Support the family culture.** Most business-owning families take great pride in the family atmosphere they have created in their businesses. They also appreciate the fact that they can promote values they hold dear– integrity, honesty, and community service, for example — through their businesses. **One of their greatest fears in hiring outsiders is that the culture of the business will be diluted and that the values it stands for will dissipate.** Be sensitive to the family's values and do what you can to help maintain the culture that it has worked hard to build. If you're the head of marketing, for example, welcome key family members to your meetings now and then to talk about family values.

Achieving success as an outsider in a family-owned company can be quite tricky. You may have to suppress your ego from time to time or bite your tongue to keep from agreeing or disagreeing when one family member complains about another. But if you are competent, professional, and trustworthy, you most likely will become a valued part of the senior management team, and the rewards will be great.

One other thought: Your ability to succeed will be greatly enhanced if you and the business owner are clear on your expectations of each other. Read the rest of this book to gain an understanding of the owner's perspective and to discover where expectations might not be clear. When they are not, you need to gather more information. If, for

> *Be sensitive to the family's values and do what you can to help maintain the culture that it has worked hard to build.*

example, the owner has put you in charge of a department that includes her son, do you know if she wants you to be more demanding of the son or to treat him just like other employees? If you don't know, you need to ask — and when you find out, you need to be sure that the owner communicates with her son about what directions she has given you as his supervisor.

Being a significant leader in a family business can result in a tremen-dously satisfying career. **The opportunity to be part of a meaningful enterprise that stands for something, the chance to make a real dif-ference and be appreciated for it, the sense of being more than another climber of a corporate ladder...can make the role of a key non-family executive in a family business one of the best opportunities available.**

IX. *Summary*

Lucky is the family business where growth is such that it needs to hire and can support the employment of executives who come from outside the family. This means the business is doing just what supporters of the free-enterprise system hopes it will do: create jobs and contribute to the economy. That should serve as a great source of pride to the business-owning family.

Nevertheless, hiring and working with non-family managers may present challenges to a family business that it has never had to face before: the loss of some privacy; the need to create career paths for talented people other than family members; and the necessity of relying on, sharing sensitive information with, and developing trusting relationships with people from outside the family.

These demands call for new behavior on the part of the family — especially family executives. To create an environment in which non-family managers can succeed and do for the business what they were brought in to do, family executives — especially the CEO — must learn to share power, delegate responsibility, and communicate openly. They must also adopt policies and practices that assure that non-family managers are treated and compensated fairly. In addition, they will find it beneficial to involve their key non-family players in strategic planning and decision-making and to use them as resources who can teach the younger members of the family and prepare them for leadership roles in the company.

These are complex processes, and families will stumble from time to time as they try to get things right. Some hires won't be the right choices after all, and a business owner may have to consciously push past the feeling of being "burned" to try again. Misunderstandings will occur — an "outsider" may think she has a shot at the top job or at ownership in the company when that's not what the business owners have in mind at all. On the whole, however, following the precepts outlined on these pages will greatly enhance a business owner's chances of working successfully with non-family executives and diminish the likelihood of making mistakes.

And, happily, the processes of hiring, managing, and retaining talented outside executives gets easier over time. The greatest difficulties occur in the first generation, when the company is small, family members aren't used to working with outsiders, and the personality of the founder — like the personality of many entrepreneurs — lends itself to being more controlling, more secretive, and less trusting than succeeding business leaders. By the second, third, or fourth generation, the family will have built a track record of working with non-family executives and have come to accept it as a natural, necessary part of running a growing, thriving business.

As difficult as it is to hire and work with those first non-family executives, doing so, by its very nature, makes the company — and the family managers — more professional. The family executives will find themselves stepping up to the excellence of the talented people they have had the intelligence to hire. And when they take full advantage of that talent by managing it wisely and well, they have power as never before to grow the company they love to the next level and the next and the next.

When that happens, many, many people benefit. The family enjoys greater wealth and more pride in their creation; the non-family executives build personal wealth and great careers for themselves; and the community prospers as more quality jobs are created in a values-strong company and the local economy strengthens.

Index

61

The Authors

Craig E. Aronoff and John L. Ward have long been recognized as leaders in the family business field. Founding principals of the **Family Business Consulting Group**, they work with hundreds of family businesses around the world. Recipients of the Family Firm Institute's Beckhard Award for outstanding contributions to family business practice, they have spoken to family business audiences on every continent. Their books include *Family Business Sourcebook* II and the three-volume series, *The Future of Private Enterprise.*

Craig E. Aronoff, Ph.D., holds the Dinos Eminent Scholar Chair of Private Enterprise and is professor of management at Kennesaw State University (Atlanta). He founded and directs the university's Family Enterprise Center. The center focuses on education and research for family businesses, and its programs have been emulated by more than 100 universities worldwide. In addition to his undergraduate degree from Northwestern University and Masters from the University of Pennsylvania, he holds a Ph.D. in organizational communication from the University of Texas.

John L. Ward, Ph.D., is Clinical Professor of Family Enterprises at Northwestern University's Kellogg Graduate School of Management. He is a regular visiting lecturer at two European business schools. He has also previously been associate dean of Loyola University Chicago's Graduate School of Business, and a senior associate with Strategic Planning Institute (PIMS Program) in Cambridge, Massachusetts. A graduate of Northwestern University (B.A) and Stanford Graduate School of Business (M.B.A. and Ph.D.), his *Keeping the Family Business Healthy* and *Creating Effective Boards for Private Enterprises* are leading books in the family business field.

The best information resources for business-owning families and their advisors

The Family Business Leadership Series
Concise guides dealing with the most pressing challenges and significant opportunities confronting family businesses.

Comprehensive — Readable — Thoroughly Practical

- *Family Business Succession: The Final Test of Greatness*
- *Family Meetings: How to Build a Stronger Family and a Stronger Business*
- *Another Kind of Hero: Preparing Successors for Leadership*
- *How Families Work Together*
- *Family Business Compensation*
- *How to Choose & Use Advisors: Getting the Best Professional Family Business Advice*
- *Financing Transitions: Managing Capital and Liquidity in the Family Business*
- *Family Business Governance: Maximizing Family and Business Potential*
- *Preparing Your Family Business for Strategic Change*
- *Making Sibling Teams Work: The Next Generation*
- *Developing Family Business Policies: Your Guide to the Future*
- *Family Business Values: How to Assure a Legacy of Continuity and Success*
- New guides on critical issues published every six to twelve months

The Family Business ADVISOR Monthly Newsletter

Family Business Sourcebook II
Edited by Drs. Aronoff and Ward with Dr. Joseph H. Astrachan, *Family Business Sourcebook II* contains the best thoughts, advice, experience and insights on the subject of family business. Virtually all of the best-known experts in the field are represented.

Now Available:
John Ward's Groundbreaking Family Business Classics
- *Keeping The Family Business Healthy*
- *Creating Effective Boards For Private Enterprises*

For more information:
Business Owner Resources, P.O. Box 4356, Marietta, GA 30061
Tel: 800-551-0633 or 770-425-6673